MOSES

ENCOUNTERING GOD

12 Studies for Individuals or Groups

GREG ASIMAKOUPOULOS

SHAW

MOSES
A SHAW BOOK
PUBLISHED BY WATERBROOK PRESS
5446 North Academy Boulevard, Suite 200
Colorado Springs, CO 80918
A division of Random House, Inc.

ISBN: 9780877885191

146502721

CONTENTS

INTRODUCTION

Many of us are familiar with the story of baby Moses hidden in the bulrushes or Moses coming down from Mount Sinai with the Ten Commandments. But sometimes the exposure we have had to childhood stories or to dramatic Hollywood portrayals of his life can have vaccination-like results, preventing us from encountering the real essence of who Moses was.

The real story about Moses is more than the simple narrative that describes his childhood. His biography is critically relevant to all those today who are sincerely seeking God and who are surrounded on every side by a morally decaying society. Why? Because Moses' day and age was strikingly similar to ours.

For three hundred and sixty years the descendants of Abraham, Isaac, and Jacob had grown up and grown old living in Egypt, far removed from the land God had promised them. Initially, because Joseph (one of Jacob's sons) was a respected leader in Egypt, the Israelites' lifestyle was reasonably comfortable. But as time went on, the successive pharaohs gradually forgot the historical context which accounted for this growing group of refugees, and the Israelites became the primary slave labor force for the Egyptian society. Cruel conditions, inhumane treatment, and infanticide broke the backs and the spirits of God's chosen race. Just as in our time, being part of God's family then meant being a minority voice in a pagan society and wondering if God was indeed in control. Enter God's man Moses.

Here is a man born into a family of faith, whose parents had a sense of God's call on his life from the beginning. But as is true for every person before and after, Moses had to discover for himself what it meant to do God's will God's way. As a friend of mine likes to say, "Moses spent the first forty years of his life thinking he was a somebody, the next forty years convinced he was a nobody, and the last forty years of his life realizing that God uses nobodies."

Here is a man whose stark encounters with God changed him forever. From the first call of God under the burning bush to shepherding God's people through the wilderness, he demonstrated through strength and weakness how to be a person of faith in all the changing seasons of life.

Here is a frustrated leader and a flawed follower of God, whose story is not at all unlike yours and mine. As I worked on this guide, I realized in a new way how Moses' struggles bore a striking resemblance to my own, and I pray that you will find that to be true for your life as well. May this brief study of Moses' life lead you to take steps, no matter how faltering, to respond to God's call as you encounter him day by day.

Just As I am

Strangely aware of a destiny tattooed upon my heart
I started out not sure of how to find God's will for me.
Aimlessly I wandered in the desert land of doubt
detoured by the desires of my unsurrendered will,
until the presence of my father's God
flamed around me, called my name.
And the shame I'd worn too long
like rags fell off of me
as humbled by his call
I fell on my face,
willing to fulfill
my now forgotten destiny.
Repenting of my pride
I confessed the fear I felt inside
and courageously
(though cautiously)
responded as I am.

Greg Asimakoupoulos

Ancient World
c.1500-1300 B.C.

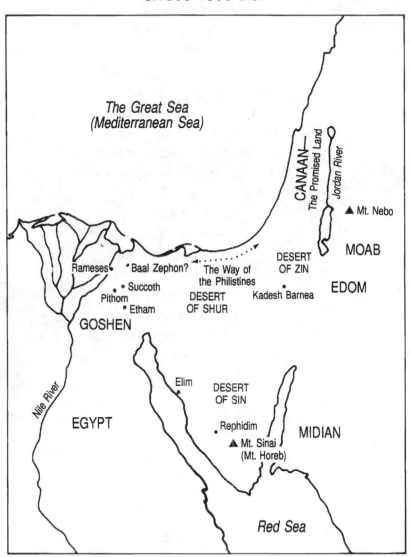

The Great Sea
(Mediterranean Sea)

CANAAN—
The Promised Land

Jordan River

▲ Mt. Nebo

MOAB

Rameses

Baal Zephon?

The Way of
the Philistines

DESERT
OF ZIN

EDOM

Succoth

Pithom

DESERT
OF SHUR

Kadesh Barnea

Etham

GOSHEN

Elim

DESERT
OF SIN

Nile River

Rephidim

MIDIAN

EGYPT

▲ Mt. Sinai
(Mt. Horeb)

Red Sea

HOW TO USE THIS STUDYGUIDE

Fisherman studyguides are based on the inductive approach to Bible study. Inductive study is discovery study; we discover what the Bible says as we ask questions about its content and search for answers. This is quite different from the process in which a teacher *tells* a group *about* the Bible and what it means and what to do about it. In inductive study God speaks directly to each of us through his Word.

A group functions best when a leader keeps the discussion on target, but this leader is neither the teacher nor the "answer person." A leader's responsibility is to *ask*—not *tell*. The answers come from the text itself as group members examine, discuss, and think together about the passage.

There are four kinds of questions in each study. The first is an *approach question*. Used before the Bible passage is read, this question breaks the ice and helps you focus on the topic of the Bible study. It begins to reveal where thoughts and feelings need to be transformed by Scripture.

Some of the earlier questions in each study are *observation questions* designed to help you find out basic facts—who, what, where, when, and how.

When you know what the Bible says you need to ask, *What does it mean?* These *interpretation questions* help you to discover the writer's basic message.

Application questions ask, *What does it mean to me?* They challenge you to live out the Scripture's life-transforming message.

Fisherman studyguides provide spaces between questions for jotting down responses and related questions you would like to raise in the group. Each group member should have a copy of the studyguide and may take a turn in leading the group.

For consistency, Fisherman guides are written from the *New International Version*. But a group should feel free to use the NIV or any other accurate, modern translation of the Bible such as the *New Living Translation*, the *New Revised Standard Version*, the *New Jerusalem Bible*, or the *Good News Bible*. (Other paraphrases of the Bible may be referred to when additional help is needed.) Bible commentaries should not be brought to a Bible study because they tend to dampen discussion and keep people from thinking for themselves.

SUGGESTIONS FOR GROUP LEADERS

1. Read and study the Bible passage thoroughly beforehand, grasping its themes and applying its teachings for yourself. Pray that the Holy Spirit will "guide you into truth" so that your leadership will guide others.

2. If the studyguide's questions ever seem ambiguous or unnatural to you, rephrase them, feeling free to add others that seem necessary to bring out the meaning of a verse.

3. Begin (and end) the study promptly. Start by asking someone to pray for God's help. Remember, the Holy Spirit is the teacher, not you!

4. Ask for volunteers to read the passages out loud.

5. As you ask the studyguide's questions in sequence, encourage everyone to participate in the discussion. If some are silent, ask,

"What do you think, Heather?" or, "Dan, what can you add to that answer?" or suggest, "Let's have an answer from someone who hasn't spoken up yet."

6. If a question comes up that you can't answer, don't be afraid to admit that you're baffled! Assign the topic as a research project for someone to report on next week.

7. Keep the discussion moving and focused. Though tangents will inevitably be introduced, you can bring the discussion back to the topic at hand. Learn to pace the discussion so that you finish a study each session you meet.

8. Don't be afraid of silences; some questions take time to answer and some people need time to gather courage to speak. If silence persists, rephrase your question, but resist the temptation to answer it yourself.

9. If someone comes up with an answer that is clearly illogical or unbiblical, ask him or her for further clarification: "What verse suggests that to you?"

10. Discourage Bible-hopping and overuse of cross-references. Learn all you can from *this* passage, along with a few important references suggested in the studyguide.

11. Some questions are marked with a ♦. This indicates that further information is available in the Leader's Notes at the back of the guide.

12. For further information on getting a new Bible study group started and keeping it functioning effectively, read Gladys Hunt's *You Can Start a Bible Study Group* and *Pilgrims in Progress: Growing through Groups* by Jim and Carol Plueddemann.

SUGGESTIONS FOR GROUP MEMBERS

1. Learn and apply the following ground rules for effective Bible study. (If new members join the group later, review these guidelines with the whole group.)

2. Remember that your goal is to learn all that you can *from the Bible passage being studied.* Let it speak for itself without using Bible commentaries or other Bible passages. There is more than enough in each assigned passage to keep your group productively occupied for one session. Sticking to the passage saves the group from insecurity and confusion.

3. Avoid the temptation to bring up those fascinating tangents that don't really grow out of the passage you are discussing. If the topic is of common interest, you can bring it up later in informal conversation following the study. Meanwhile, help each other stick to the subject!

4. Encourage each other to participate. People remember best what they discover and verbalize for themselves. Some people are naturally shier than others, or they may be afraid of making a mistake. If your discussion is free and friendly and you show real interest in what other group members think and feel, they will be more likely to speak up. Remember, the more people involved in a discussion, the richer it will be.

5. Guard yourself from answering too many questions or talking too much. Give others a chance to express themselves. If you are one who participates easily, discipline yourself by counting to ten before you open your mouth!

6. Make personal, honest applications and commit yourself to letting God's Word change you.

A CHILD OF PROVIDENCE

Exodus 1:1–2:10; Acts 7:17-22

At some point in life, most of us reflect on the ultimate issues: Where did I come from? Why am I here? Where am I going? Is God really in control? We struggle to come up with answers when life presses in and we doubt our significance. But according to the Bible, those questions do have answers. God has known us from the time we were being knit together in our mothers' wombs (Psalm 139); he knows the length of our life even before we take an initial breath; he knows our destiny.

Moses came on the scene at a particularly difficult time for God's people. They were asking some ultimate questions too. Yet, even before Moses was conciously aware of his role as a son or leader, his life was being providentially choreographed by the Lord. In his example we find courage to trust God to clarify the meaning of our lives too.

1. Describe the circumstances of your family surrounding your birth, as you understand them. What was going on in the lives of your parents and siblings as you entered the world?

Read Exodus 1:1-22.

♦ **2.** What accounted for the new king's negative attitude toward the Israelites?

3. Describe the measures he took to control the Israelites (verses 11-16, 22)? What motivated these actions?

4. What impresses you about the Hebrew midwives? Why did they do what they did?

In what situations do you feel civil disobedience justifies breaking the law of the land? Explain.

Read Exodus 2:1-10.

5. By what means did Moses' parents attempt to preserve his life?

6. Put yourself in their shoes for a moment. What might have been their reasoning with this plan? (Compare 1:22; see also Hebrews 11:23.)

7. How did Moses' sister participate in this scenario of grace?

8. Observe Pharaoh's daughter in verses 5-10. How do her actions and character compare with that of her father's?

9. Ultimately the princess adopted Moses. What are some of the special issues that adopted children might deal with, including Moses?

Read Acts 7:17-22.

10. What more do we learn about Moses' birth from this passage?

11. Even as a baby, Moses was a "child of privilege." How did Moses continue to benefit from being raised in the household of Pharaoh?

♦ **12.** What evidences of God's intervention do you see in the circumstances surrounding Moses' birth?

Looking back, what examples of God's providence in your life can you recount?

A MIDLIFE CRISIS AND RENEWED CALL

Exodus 2:11–3:10

The world today is quite a different place than it was when Moses donned his royal Egyptian robes. But some things have not changed that much. Sin continues to erode the human soul. The cycle of life and death goes on. And often at the mid-way point in life, people still wrestle with regrets, mortality, and spiritual ambivalence.

In this study, Moses is forty years old and he is challenged by the same concerns. As God encounters this displaced prince, dethroned of his pride in a rather unexpected way, a new season in the life of Moses begins. Here we see a picture of how God seeks out those too weak to trust themselves. Moses' midlife crisis is instructive to all who would understand how to deal with the uncertainties of life and faith regardless of their age.

◆ **1.** At this point in your life, what would you say has been one of your greatest achievements, personally or professionally? What has been one of your main regrets?

Read Exodus 2:11-22.

2. What clues do you see in these verses that Moses was aware of his Hebrew roots?

How do you think he felt about his heritage? Explain your answer.

◆ **3.** Explore Pharaoh's reaction to Moses' behavior. What does this say about his relationship to his adopted son?

4. What more do you learn about Moses and this situation from Acts 7:23-29?

Do you see any reason to believe that his flight was more than just running scared?

◆ **5.** How would you explain Moses' sense of destiny to be a deliverer of God's people? Why was this self-awareness not validated by his peers?

◆ **6.** If you had been one of Reuel's daughters, how would you have described Moses? How did they know he was an Egyptian (verses 16-19)?

7. Identify all the changes and losses that Moses experienced in this period. How does he cope with it all (verses 21-22)?

Have you ever felt like Moses? If so, how did you handle it?

Read Exodus 2:23–3:10.

◆ **8.** While Moses was tending flocks and raising a family, what was happening back in Egypt (2:23-25)?

◆ **9.** What prompted Moses to investigate the bush on Mount Horeb?

How is the voice from the bush identified (verses 2-4)?

10. Why do you think God makes the three opening statements he does to Moses in this extraordinary encounter (verses 5-6)? What do they reveal that Moses would have needed to know?

11. Find all the verbs in verses 7-8 which are associated with God. What kind of God do these words reveal?

12. What new call was Moses given at the mid-point of his life? What hope did God offer for the future?

13. Elizabeth Barrett Browning wrote: "Earth is crammed with heaven and every bush afire with God. But only those who see take off their shoes." What can you do this week to slow down and listen to what God may be asking you to do?

A MOST RELUCTANT LEADER

Exodus 3:11–4:17

My father-in-law was a most unlikely candidate to succeed in life. Deposited in an orphanage as a two-year-old by his unwed mother, he was eventually adopted, but grew up feeling rejected and unloved. He never went to college. When he felt God's call to become a missionary, he knew he was sorely lacking in the necessary skills. But he and his wife took the risk and joined up with Wycliffe Bible Translators. In the forty years since, my father-in-law has written thirty books and distinguished himself as Wycliffe's foremost biographer and historian.

Moses, too, was adopted, but unlike my father-in-law, Moses' royal upbringing and education provided every reason to feel self-assured as a leader and a spokesman. But Moses' self-confidence soon evaporated during his forty-year assignment as a shepherd in Midian. As a result, God's call to lead his people out of Egypt was muffled by the sound of Moses' pounding, anxious heart.

1. What is one of your phobias or fears? Do you have a logical explanation why you feel afraid in that given context?

Read Exodus 3:11-22.

2. What is Moses' response to God's call?

Given what you understand of Moses' life thus far, does his reaction surprise you? Why or why not?

3. God counters Moses' concerns with a promise and a sign. What are they?

4. For Moses, the LORD was the same God of his great ancestors, Abraham, Isaac, and Jacob. As you contemplate your spiritual roots, what names would you use as a point of reference and examples of faith?

♦ **5.** How does God further identify himself in answer to Moses' question (verses 13-15)?

Why did Moses think he would have to identify God more specifically to the Israelites?

6. Identify the two steps of God's intended deliverance (verses 16-18). Which aspect of this mission would be more desirable had you been Moses? Why?

Read Exodus 4:1-17.

7. Insecure once again, Moses begins a litany of "what ifs." How does the Lord respond to Moses' question in verse 1 (compare with 3:18)?

8. What was God's purpose in using the object lessons of the snake and the leprosy (verses 3-9)?

What did Moses' staff represent in his life?

9. How does God eloquently demonstrate to this stutterer the irrelevancy of his next complaint (verses 10-12)?

10. Amazingly, Moses still resists. What is God's alternative plan?

Has God ever put an "Aaron" in your life to compensate for your areas of weakness? Explain.

11. Look at all the "I will" promises God gives to Moses in these passages. How do you respond to the fact that God is determined to accomplish his goals in our lives even when we balk?

12. What can you take away from this study to help you face situations in which you feel totally inadequate?

FACING A DIFFICULT EMPLOYER

Exodus 5:1–6:12

If you are unhappy in your job, you are not alone. It is a documented fact that most people don't enjoy what they do for a living. The reasons given for discontentment range from commute time to lack of a personal challenge to unethical practices. For Christians in the marketplace, dressing faith in work clothes can be difficult. This is especially true if they work for an insensitive employer who does not recognize their abilities or esteem their values.

This study offers a peek at Moses' attempt to obey God while confronted with a capricious "employer," Pharaoh, who was determined to outsmart God's servant. What Moses did to remain true to his calling and convictions is instructive to anyone who routinely must face a less than perfect work environment. He reminds us that our primary identity or source of fulfillment is not in our careers.

1. On a scale of one to ten (ten being greatly satisfied), how would you rate your current job satisfaction? Why?

Read Exodus 5:1-23.

♦ **2.** After meeting with the Israelite elders, Moses and Aaron go to Pharaoh. Who do they credit as the author of their request?

Why should a request by Israel's God even matter to Pharaoh?

3. How does Moses and Aaron's second request differ from the first (verses 1 and 3)?

Does their rationale to persuade Pharaoh a second time strike you as odd (compare with Exodus 3:18)? How so?

4. What do Pharaoh's reactions reveal about his character and his priorities (verses 2, 4-5, 8-9)?

5. Trace the chain reaction of events once Moses confronts Pharaoh. How does Pharaoh make life more difficult for the Israelites? for the foremen? for Moses and Aaron?

6. To whom does Moses turn when Pharaoh doesn't respond? What strong feelings are underneath Moses' prayer?

Who are you inclined to talk with when things go wrong?

Read Exodus 6:1-12.

7. Paraphrase the main points of the Lord's response to Moses' prayer of frustration.

How does God reassure Moses over and over that he is still involved in the situation?

◆ 8. By what name had God made himself known to Moses' ancestors?

How would Moses' knowledge of this more personal name for God make him feel?

9. List the marvelous promises the Lord makes to the Israelites in spite of Pharaoh's defiant attitude.

10. What precluded Moses' colleagues from listening to his update?

11. Analyze Moses' logic in verse 12. How would you have answered him if you had been the Lord?

12. If you can, describe a time when discouragement or tough breaks have kept you from believing God's promises. Why was it hard to trust God during those times? Pray for strength and faith as you deal with difficult relationships and situations.

A STUDENT OF FAITH

Exodus 13:17–14:31; Hebrews 11:23-28

"Lord, give me patience and give it to me now!" Such a prayer is a comic reminder of how easy it is to resist the hard lessons in life that actually serve to develop our faith muscles. We think we want to learn how to incorporate more patience, more love, more faith into our lives, until we realize what the tuition costs of such an education really are.

I don't know about you, but the university I attended didn't offer a course on faith (and it was a Chrisian school). It's just not a subject that can be taught in a classroom. We are only enrolled in the school of faith through a free gift by God himself (Ephesians 2:8), but mastering the subject requires a lifetime of spiritual homework and tests. In chapter 11 of Hebrews, Moses is listed as one of several honor roll students who completed the course of faith with flying colors. Though not perfect, his example encourages us and reminds us that the lessons of faith are always worth the cost.

1. Do you consider yourself a good student in the school of faith? Why or why not?

Read Exodus 13:17–14:9.

◆ **2.** Trace on the map (p. 8) the escape route of the Israelites (13:17-18, 20; 14:1-2). Why does God choose this less obvious route?

3. What does Moses take with him from Egypt? In what way was his insistence on taking this sacred cargo a symbolic expression of faith (see also Genesis 50:24-25)?

◆ **4.** How does God's itinerary mislead Pharaoh's army?

In what way did it force the Israelites to trust God?

Read Exodus 14:10-31.

♦ **5.** Compare the initial reaction of the hemmed-in Israelites with Moses' response to this serious situation (verses 10-13). Based on your experience, what is the relationship between fear and faith?

♦ **6.** According to verses 29-31, what accounted for the Israelites' change of heart?

7. What do you observe of Moses' growing relationship with God during this event?

Read Hebrews 11:23-28.

8. How would Pharaoh's edict have challenged the parent's belief that their son had a special calling on his life?

Did they hide him because they believed he was special or simply because they wanted to spare his life? In what way was this an exercise of faith for them?

9. Why did Moses willingly deny himself treasure and pleasure?

In the school of faith, was this a basic course or a graduate level course for Moses? Why?

10. Think about the benefits—material and spiritual—you have inherited growing up in North America. Do benefits like these tend to fuel faith or minimize it? Discuss.

11. Can you identify one or more ways your decision to take your faith seriously has cost you? What are they?

12. What can you deliberately do to "home school" your children or other young people in the ABCs of faith?

A GRATEFUL SON-IN-LAW

Exodus 18

In-law jokes are rampant, and they are funny in part because they reflect the reality that these relationships are often less than humorous. I know from my years of pastoring that the dynamics of in-law relationships can be challenging at best and nearly impossible at worst. But when they are good, they can be a great source of wisdom and perspective. I'm grateful for a father-in-law who has often provided encouragement to me and my family.

Moses, too, was blessed with a father-in-law who took an active interest in his life work. Because Moses was willing to accept Jethro's counsel, his effectiveness increased exponentially.

1. What in-law has enriched your life as much as any family member? Describe the contributions he or she has made.

Read Exodus 18:1-12.

◆ **2.** What do we learn about Moses' family here? Why did Jethro visit Moses?

3. Note how Moses welcomes his father-in-law. Do you detect more than a cultural cordiality in this gesture? If so, what does this show about their relationship?

4. Describe the ways Jethro responds to Moses' testimony to the Lord's faithfulness.

Does his response surprise you? Why or why not?

Read Exodus 18:13-27.

♦ **5.** What is Moses' work situation like? What pressures would there be?

How do you think this job evolved for Moses?

6. When asked for an explanation of his approach, what is implied in Moses' rationale?

7. Paraphrase Jethro's response to what he was seeing. What is his motivation for this advice (verses 14-23)?

8. What were the benefits for Moses and the Israelites inherent in Jethro's suggested managament model? What were the costs? Explain.

9. How could this model work in the corporate world today? in the church?

10. What about Moses' actions in verses 24-26 stands out to you as important? Why? How could he have responded?

11. When the effects of stress and burn out affect your ability to effectively serve those around you, what can you do to safeguard yourself from workaholism?

12. How can you support and encourage each other in the tasks you face this week?

A MAN OF PASSIONS

Exodus 32:1-6; 15-35; Numbers 20:1-13

Isn't it amazing who Jesus chose to be his apostles? James and John were hotheaded. Peter was impetuous. Matthew had a checkered past. Judas was deceitful. But when you stop and think about it, God has always chosen imperfect persons for significant assignments. King David was guilty of sexual sin and pre-meditated murder. Before his conversion, the apostle Paul was an ego-driven bounty hunter determined to annihilate Christians.

And then there was Moses. The cooing infant in the makeshift waterproof cradle grew up to become anything but a calm, even-tempered adult. He was a hostage of his anger much of his life. Still, he was God's choice to lead the chosen people from slavery into freedom. Do you ever wonder if your past failures or present weaknesses disqualify you as a leader in the kingdom of God? This study will challenge the perception that we have to be nearly perfect in order to be effective in God's service.

1. With what biblical character do you most easily identify in terms of temperament, personality, and passion? Why?

Read Exodus 32:1-6.

2. Moses had been on Mount Sinai with God for some time, receiving the commandments. Describe the Israelites' response to Moses' absence. What about their comments suggests disrepect?

♦ **3.** What do you think was Aaron's reasoning behind his actions?

What is ironic about his instructions to the people (verses 4-5)?

Read Exodus 32:15-35.

4. As Moses and Joshua came down from the mountain with the tablets from God, what were their reactions to what they heard and saw?

Do you think Moses' anger got the best of him and he went overboard? Why or why not?

5. Relate the immediate actions which Moses took as if you were a news reporter on the scene, describing "who, what, where, when, why" (verses 25-29).

What motivated this harsh response?

6. After sleeping on it, how does Moses' approach to the disobedient Israelites change (verse 30)?

What in Moses' actions signals a heart (albeit flawed by undisciplined passions) that still feared God?

Read Numbers 20:1-13.

◆ **7.** Later, as the Israelites journeyed in the wilderness, what difficulties was Moses forced to face?

Which of these challenges would have been hardest for you to handle? Why?

8. What is stated in the Israelites' litany of complaints? What is implied?

9. To where did Moses and Aaron turn in this crisis?

Does this response surprise you? Why or why not?

♦ **10.** God once again assures Moses of his provision for the people's needs, yet in what ways does Moses violate God's directions?

What is the result of Moses' disobedience for the Israelites? for himself?

♦ **11.** How does it help you to know that a godly person like Moses struggled with an uncontrollable temper?

12. What do you learn from these events in Moses' life about how to handle crises and express anger appropriately?

LIFE-CHANGING ENCOUNTERS

Exodus 19:1-13; 33:7-23

The popularity of seminars and books dealing with spirituality clearly indicates an unprecedented spiritual hunger in our culture. Life devoid of mystery lacks color and is one-dimensional. Human beings long for an experience of the supernatural. This is the way our transcendent God has wired us. Such a God does not then hide from us, but seeks us out.

Moses had some life-changing encounters of the supernatural kind on several occasions. Each time, God initiated the meeting and Moses responded. We also have the challenge of learning to recognize those moments when God comes calling and then embracing the mystery of his holy presence.

1. In what setting are you most aware of the mystery and glory of God's presence? Is there a correlation with that place and where you gather for public worship? Why or why not?

Read Exodus 19:1-13.

♦ **2.** Before Moses hears the Lord call him, what does he do?

3. In his initial encounter with the Lord, Moses received instruction from God. What are the highlights of God's message to the Israelites?

♦ **4.** What does the word picture used in verse 4 convey about the Lord and his activity among his people? Where does he bring the Israelites?

Is this an appropriate picture of the way God has dealt with you at times in your life? If so, how?

5. What patterns of communication do you observe in this encounter between Moses and God?

What can this suggest about our prayer time with the Lord?

6. What in these verses indicates the manner in which Moses and the people were to approach the Lord?

How can we accommodate this call to reverence in our day?

Read Exodus 33:7-23.

♦ **7.** According to this passage, what was the purpose of the tent of meeting?

8. Curiously, when Moses went to encounter the Lord at the tent of meeting, where did the people worship?

What does this suggest about God's accessibility to us? about where we can worship?

9. How does the Lord speak to Moses in the tent of meeting? Identify aspects of communication enjoyed by friends.

10. Based on verse 12, the Lord had already communicated some things to Moses. What further concerns does Moses have? How does God respond?

11. Describe the elements of approachability versus holy separation that characterize God in these encounters with Moses (verses 9, 11, 14, 17, 19-20).

12. If you were absolutely convinced the Lord knew you by name and was pleased with you, how would that knowledge affect your relationship with him? with others in your life?

A VEILED MEDIATOR

Exodus 34:27-35; 2 Corinthians 3:4-18

When I was a small boy, my mother always knew when I had done something wrong. I just looked guilty, she said. Even when I tried to mislead her with my explanations, the truth was written all over my face.

In a similar way, it was no secret to the people of Israel when Moses had been with God. His face gave him away. However, unlike me, his visage didn't reveal guilt and shame. As the chosen mediator between God and his people, Moses' face reflected a loving God who was tangibly involved in their journey to the Land of Promise.

1. When we are spending time in Bible study and prayer, what do you think others might see in us that would indicate we've been with the Lord?

Read Exodus 34:27-35.

    2. How does Moses spend these forty days with God (see also 34:4-9)?

    3. As he comes down from meeting with the Lord on Mount Sinai, what does he carry in his hands? What does he carry on his face?

    4. What results from this display of radiance?

    ♦ **5.** Describe the pattern that dictates the use of the veil. Why do you think Moses veiled his face?

♦ **6.** In spite of his appearance, what does Moses continue to pass on to the people?

What insight has the Lord recently helped you see in his Word or through prayerful reflection that might benefit someone else?

Read 2 Corinthians 3:4-18.

♦ **7.** The apostle Paul is defending his ministry to the church at Corinth in this passage. From this passage, how would you define the "new covenant" to which Paul refers?

8. According to this account, what was part of Moses' motive for wearing a veil over his face?

Why would he not want people to see the glory fade?

9. How does Paul account for the spiritual blindness of those outside of Christ (verses 14-15)?

Do you think the metaphor of a veil is an appropriate one? Why or why not?

10. When someone turns to the Lord, what things occur (verses 16-18)?

11. How would you characterize Paul's attitude toward those before whom he lives out his faith?

Which of these attributes do you most desire as Christ continues his spiritual transformation in you?

12. Think back on Moses' encounter with the Lord on Mount Sinai, away from the crowd. How can you structure your day to allow for an uninterrupted time of worship and prayer in a private place? Share what works for you.

A MAN OF GOD

Psalm 90

The famous quoter Anonymous has said, "People tend to worship their work, work at their play, and play at their worship." For many Christians today, godliness is often squeezed out with busyness. Fortunately, God has regularly called out men and women to raise the standard of commitment in their generation. Moses was such a person.

As Moses entered the autumn of his life, he reflected on the core values of his faith. He was aware of God's hand in his life. He knew he had a message to relay to future generations. One of his prayers has been preserved for us in Psalm 90. Here we see a godly man who paints a colorful still-life picture of God's holiness and our finiteness.

1. Who is the most godly person you have ever met? What qualifies him or her for this place in your mind?

Read Psalm 90.

    2. Reflecting on this psalm as a whole, what emotional peaks and valleys in Moses' prayer do you see?

    3. Using verses 1-2 as a point of reference, describe all the qualities of God with which Moses had become acquainted.

What would this knowledge of God have meant to you if you had been wandering in the desert for years?

    4. Compare God's perspective of time with ours. How do you feel about the speed with which life passes?

◆ **5.** What in verses 7 and 8 indicates Moses' sensitivity to God's holiness?

What hope is there for sinners who are scrutinized by the search light of an all-seeing God?

6. How is Moses' realism seen in this portrait of human life he has painted?

Do you agree with his general description of life? Why or why not?

7. Describe what you think "numbering our days" involves (verse 12)?

Why would wisdom be a by-product of such an activity?

8. In his role as mediator for God's people, what further requests does Moses make of the Lord in verses 13-17?

What words here stand out as hopes you long for in this season in your life?

9. Review what you know of Moses' life and his early reluctance to obey God. How has his view of God changed since then? What accounts for this growth?

10. Thinking back to your answer to question 1, what made Moses a godly person?

11. What have you learned about God and his actions from Moses' prayer that encourages you most right now?

A LASTING LEGACY

Deuteronomy 5:1–6:12; 30:11–31:6

Visit a cemetery and you'll find tombstones of all shapes and sizes showing the deceased's date of birth and date of death, separated by a small, insignificant hyphen—as if a little dash could represent the legacy of a whole life. Fortunately, what we leave behind for those who survive us isn't limited to the space on a grave marker. Our values, beliefs, choices, and spiritual investments are timeless gifts we can bequeath our family and friends.

As Moses came to the close of his life, he too, left a valuable legacy, not only for his generation but for every generation since. It included the Ten Commandments, God's moral law, and encouraging words about the faithfulness of God.

1. What would you like to be remembered for after you die?

Read Deuteronomy 5:1-22.

2. In this chapter Moses is recounting highlights of the Israelites' experiences with God on Mount Horeb. What were the Israelites to do with the information Moses gave them? Why (verses 1-5)?

3. What can you infer about the importance of what was to follow from God's opening statement in verse 6?

♦ **4.** What relational categories do the commandments seem to fall into? Are they equally weighted in terms of their importance? Explain your answer.

Read Deuteronomy 5:32–6:12.

6. List all the benefits, stated and implied, of following God's commands.

7. Was the Israelites' obedience to God an attempt to gain his favor, to express gratitude, or other? Explain.

8. In what ways are the people to pass on knowledge of God's Word to the next generation?

What contemporary ways can you think of to accomplish the intent of these orginal suggestions?

9. In light of the future hope God offered, why is Moses' caution not to forget the Lord appropriate (verses 3, 10-12)?

Read Deuteronomy 30:11–31:6.

10. How does Moses encourage the people with regard to their ability to honor God?

11. According to 30:15 and 19, what is the bottom line of obedience? Do you agree that it is that simple? Why or why not?

♦ **12.** Realizing he would die soon, what promises were at the core of the legacy Moses left the people of Israel (31:3-6)?

In what ways has the reality of these truths encouraged you recently?

13. Think of one or two insights you have gleaned from life experience that you would like to pass on to those who will come after you. Pray for each other to that end.

A FINAL PROMISED LAND

Deuteronomy 32:48-52; 34:1-12

If you stood on Mount Nebo in the Middle East today, you would catch a glimpse of the same beautiful hills of Canaan west of the Jordan River that, centuries ago, Moses strained his eyes to see. Yet, after faithfully leading the Israelites for forty years in the wilderness, he was denied entrance into the Promised Land. This was a bittersweet reminder of the consequences of sin in his life.

Though he wasn't able to reach the land "flowing with milk and honey," he did taste the fruit of God's ultimate promise. When Moses died, he entered into the eternal presence of the One whose voice first spoke to him from the unextinguishable bush. His final promised land had been reached.

1. Think about a special place you have always wanted to visit, but probably never will. What other blessings in your life have more than compensated for this unfulfilled longing?

64

Read Deuteronomy 32:48-52.

2. Following his vibrant song of praise and final words to the Israelites, what instructions does Moses receive?

3. Locate Mount Nebo on the map. How close would Moses come to the Promised Land?

♦ **4.** Why was Moses prevented from going with the Israelites into Canaan?

What do you think upholding God's holiness means? Why was it so important then, and now?

5. Even though this was not "news" to Moses, how do you think he might have felt about being reminded that he would be denied entrance?

Do you feel God was justified in enforcing the punishment that was triggered by Moses' earlier rage? Why?

Read Deuteronomy 34:1-12.

6. What does Moses' obedience in actually climbing Mount Nebo imply about the essence of this flawed leader?

7. Do you find anything in these verses that points to the graciousness of God? Explain.

◆ **8.** Although Moses wasn't allowed to enter the Promised Land, his life on "this side of Jordan" still had been enriched by God's promises. What promises from God *had* come true for Moses?

9. Moses had a man in place to take over for him when he died. What do you know about Joshua based on these verses alone?

10. Moses' life was not without flaws and failings. How do you account for this remarkable closing eulogy (verses 10-12)?

11. What do you admire most about Moses? Why?

12. How has this overview of Moses' life enriched your understanding of God?

13. What insights have you gleaned from this study which you can incorporate into your journey of faith right now?

LEADER'S NOTES

◼ Study 1/A Child of Providence

Question 2. Since Joseph, the Israelites had been in Egypt for nearly 400 years. The date here was probably early in the thirteenth or fourteenth centuries B.C.

Question 12. God's intervention and providence is seen in countless ways and details. Encourage your group to search these out. For example, the Hebrew name *Moses* means "to draw out." In one sense, Pharaoh's daughter drew the infant Moses out of a vulnerable situation and placed him in a God-ordained setting of security. Here he would providentially be prepared for his divine assignment later in his life.

In addition, Moses' adoption entitled him to all the rights of royalty. Although his parents had a sense their son was no ordinary child, Moses knew firsthand what it meant to be prince of the Nile. God had opened the doors of circumstance wide enough for him to enter the library of entitlement. Here he would absorb the wisdom of the world that would in time serve God's greater purpose.

◼ Study 2/A Midlife Crisis and Renewed Call

Question 1. These can be very personal questions. You may want to suggest that if anyone is uncomfortable sharing, they can feel free to think about or write down their answers in private.

Question 3. You may want to pose this additional question to your group: "Did Pharaoh know all along that his daughter's child was in fact a Hebrew? If so, what implications might that have had?"

Question 5. Apparently Moses was ready to come to terms with his Hebrew identity and stand up for his people even though it meant giving up a very profitable future under Pharaoh.

Question 6. The Hebrew word for *priest* in Exodus 2:16 could just as easily mean "chief." The name *Reuel* means "friend of God." Later in Exodus 3:1, Moses' father-in-law is called Jethro, which quite possibly was a title meaning "his excellency."

Question 8. Most scholars agree that the burning bush incident most likely happened after another forty years in Midian.

Question 9. Mount Horeb is the same mountain later referred to as Sinai. It is called the "mountain of God" because this is where the Lord repeatedly revealed himself to Moses. Have the group locate this place on the map on page 8.

The "angel of the LORD" in Exodus 3:2 was a manifestation of the LORD (Exodus 3:4-5). The intended meaning here is that this was in fact God himself engaging Moses in conversation.

■ Study 3/A Most Reluctant Leader

Question 5. In Hebrew, names signified the real personality of the person. The Hebrew name for God, *Yahweh,* is usually translated as "the LORD" or "Jehovah." *Yahweh* comes from the Hebrew tetragrammaton YHWH, used when God's name was considered too sacred to pronounce.

God's answer of "I AM" in Exodus 3:14 is the Hebrew word *'ehyeh*. "By this Moses would not think that God was announcing a *new* name; . . . it is just the inner meaning of the name Moses already knew. Here we have a play on words; 'Yahweh' is interpreted by *'ehyeh*, . . . and means 'I will be as I will be'" (*The New Bible Dictionary*, 2nd edition, J. D. Douglas, ed., p. 430. Downers Grove, Ill.: InterVarsity Press, 1994).

■ Study 4/Facing a Difficult Employer

Question 2. This was a new pharaoh, since Moses' stepfather had since died (Exodus 2:23). No exact dates are known of these events. Traditionally many scholars have believed that the fifteenth century Egyptian King Thutmose III was the pharaoh of the oppressive slavery, and his son, Amunhotep II, was the pharaoh of the exodus (c.1400 B.C.). Others believe that the later thirteenth century King Seti I and his son Rameses II, were the rulers during the Israelite oppression and exodus (c.1200 B.C.). Regardless, the new pharaoh was as unjust and hardhearted as his father.

The religion of the Eyptians at this time was spiritualized nature worship centered around the sun and the Nile River, their two sources of life, as well as other deities.

Question 8. There are many different Hebrew names for God used in the Old Testament. Two of these are used here: *God Almighty* (El Shaddai), and *the* LORD (Yahweh), which is the most sacred name for God which he himself revealed. Others are *God* (Elohim, the Creator-Sustainer), and LORD (Adonai, Master.)

■ Study 5/A Student of Faith

Question 2. Precise locations of many of these ancient sites is not known. The Israelites fled past the Egyptian border posts, through the Red Sea, and into the desert. Early theories say the exodus ocurred around 1446 B.C., later theories say around 1300-1200 B.C.

Question 4. God's knowledge of the Israelites' situation and Pharaoh's response allowed him a larger perspective. The Israelites were forced to trust him when they couldn't understand everything.

Question 5. It is obvious that the Lord wanted to demonstrate to the Israelites who was in charge here. This battle was his. See also 1 Samuel 17:47 and 2 Chronicles 20:15.

Question 6. The exact crossing place through the Red Sea, or the *Yam Suph,* the "Sea of Reeds," is unknown. (See Exodus 15:4, 22)

■ Study 6/A Grateful Son-In-Law

Question 2. Moses had two sons, Gershom and Eliezer, by his wife Zipporah. He had passed on the Hebrew custom of circumcision to her as implied in Exodus 4:24-26. It appears that after the defeat of the Amalekites, Moses sent his wife and sons to Midian to give his father-in-law a first-hand account of God's deliverance.

Question 5. The Israelites had come to view Moses as a symbol of God's presence in their midst. After all, when God acted, it was through Moses' activity. Moses had brought the people through thick and thin. Though they often railed against him, they knew they needed him.

■ Study 7/A Man of Passions

Question 3: Aaron was a people-pleasing leader, unlike his brother Moses. This event reveals all the more why God chose

Moses. It was particularly ironic and sacrilegious for Aaron to set up an altar of worship "to the Lord" in front of a golden idol. This is an apt picture of their attempt to live unconsecrated lives.

Question 7. Numbers 20:1 says "In the first month . . ." It is critical to realize that this series of events occurred forty years after the Exodus from Eygpt, not just a month following their escape. "The year is not given but a comparison with Numbers 33:38 leads to the conclusion that this chapter begins in the fortieth year after the exodus" (*The NIV Study Bible*, p. 219, Grand Rapids, Mich.: Zondervan, 1985).

Question 10: Moses' staff was more than a stick or a symbol of his profession as a shepherd; it also symbolized his call to ministry. From the time of the burning bush, this staff was a tangible reminder of God's power in his life to do all God promised. It's interesting that even though Moses blew it, God still provided water for his people. Sin doesn't necessarily block God's love from getting through.

Question 11. Have your group explore the meaning of Paul's statement in Ephesians 4:26, "In your anger do not sin."

■ Study 8/Life-Changing Encounters

Question 2. Mount Sinai is where Moses had his burning bush experience too. It was "one of the most sacred locations in Israel's history. . . . Here God made his covenant with Israel and gave his people the laws and guidelines for right living" (*Life Application Bible*, p. 134, Wheaton, Ill.: Tyndale House, 1991).

Question 4. God tenderly and strongly carried them through immense trials and brought them to himself. The presence of the Lord is always our "home base." When Jesus appointed the disciples in Mark 3, he first called them to "be with him," and then he sent them out to minister on his behalf.

Question 7. The tent of meeting was a precursor of the more durable tabernacle. It symbolized the place of God's presence in the camp. The tent of meeting was not in the center of the camp, but on the outskirts of the community.

■ Study 9/A Veiled Mediator

Question 5. Moses was not aware of his appearance. He was focused on the Lord and thus oblivious to superficial (or superfacial) concerns. Yet, profound personal spiritual experiences like his are often misunderstood and feared by others. Perhaps Moses veiled his face so that the people would not be distracted and could really hear God's words. We will see later in the study more of his motivation in 2 Corinthians 3:17-18.

Question 6. Moses' experiences with God were not meant to be an end in themselves. This is a universal principle of the Bible that we first see in Genesis 12:2-3. God blesses us to be a source of blessing to others. Israel was that nation of blessing by which the world would be blessed with salvation. Our experiences of faith are not to be enjoyed and forgotten. They are to be a means of sharing God's love and power with others.

Question 7. The old covenant (symbolized by the Ten Commandments given at Mount Sinai) was chiseled on stone tablets. It suggested a system of animal sacrifice whereby those who were guilty of breaking the laws could be forgiven. The result of this old covenant was death, since no one could keep all the regulations on their own.

The new covenant, on the other hand, (as predicted by Jeremiah 31:31-34) is one that is written on the human heart of those who have through faith received Christ's once-for-all sacrifice for sin. This is the covenant of eternal life.

◼ Study 10/A Man of God

Question 5. See 1 John 1:7-9 where we are promised forgiveness of sins when we confess and bring them into God's healing light.

◼ Study 11/A Lasting Legacy

Question 4. Discuss how the first five commands address our relationship to God and the last five address our relationship to our neighbors. Compare with Jesus' command to love God and our neighbor in Mark 12:29-31.

Question 12. See Numbers 20:9-12 for the incident of Moses' disobedience which led to being forbidden to enter the Promised Land.

◼ Study 12/A Final Promised Land

Question 4. Review the background to God's punishment of Moses in Numbers 20:1-13. The word *holiness* in Hebrew means "set apart for a sacred purpose," and "uniquely different." Against a backdrop of pagan nations whose worship of animate and inanimate objects skewed the meaning of holiness, God insists that his holy character be esteemed with reverence and obedience.

Question 8. God promised to go before Moses when he sent him to Pharaoh. He promised to display his power through the plagues. He promised to deliver the Israelites from slavery. He promised deliverance from every imaginable bondage they would face enroute to Canaan. Most of all God promised that his presence would go with Moses at all times (see Exodus 33:12-23). The fulfillment of this great promise of his presence with Moses became a point of reference for the people of Israel forever after, "As I was with Moses, so I will be with you" (Joshua 1:5).

WHAT SHOULD WE STUDY NEXT?

To help your group answer that question, we've listed the
Fisherman Guides by category so you can choose your next study.

TOPICAL STUDIES

Angels, Wright

Becoming Women of Purpose,
Barton

Building Your House on the Lord,
Brestin

Discipleship, Reapsome

Doing Justice, Showing Mercy,
Wright

Encouraging Others, Johnson

Examining the Claims of Jesus,
Brestin

Friendship, Brestin

The Fruit of the Spirit, Briscoe

Great Doctrines of the Bible,
Board

Great Passages of the Bible,
Plueddemann

Great Prayers of the Bible,
Plueddemann

**Growing Through Life's
Challenges,** Reapsome

Guidance & God's Will, Stark

Heart Renewal, Goring

Higher Ground, Brestin

Lifestyle Priorities, White

Marriage, Stevens

Miracles, Castleman

Moneywise, Larsen

One Body, One Spirit, Larsen

The Parables of Jesus, Hunt

Prayer, Jones

The Prophets, Wright

Proverbs & Parables, Brestin

Satisfying Work, Stevens &
Schoberg

Senior Saints, Reapsome

Sermon on the Mount, Hunt

Spiritual Warfare, Moreau

The Ten Commandments,
Briscoe

Who Is God? Seemuth

Who Is the Holy Spirit?
Knuckles & Van Reken

Who Is Jesus? Van Reken

Witnesses to All the World,
Plueddemann

Worship, Sibley

BIBLE BOOK STUDIES

Genesis, Fromer & Keyes

Job, Klug

Psalms, Klug

Proverbs: Wisdom That Works, Wright

Ecclesiastes, Brestin

Jonah, Habakkuk, & Malachi, Fromer & Keyes

Matthew, Sibley

Mark, Christensen

Luke, Keyes

John: Living Word, Kuniholm

Acts 1-12, Christensen

Paul (Acts 13-28), Christensen

Romans: The Christian Story, Reapsome

1 Corinthians, Hummel

Strengthened to Serve (2 Corinthians), Plueddemann

Galatians, Titus & Philemon, Kuniholm

Ephesians, Baylis

Philippians, Klug

Colossians, Shaw

Letters to the Thessalonians, Fromer & Keyes

Letters to Timothy, Fromer & Keyes

Hebrews, Hunt

James, Christensen

1 & 2 Peter, Jude, Brestin

How Should a Christian Live? (1, 2 & 3 John), Brestin

Revelation, Hunt

BIBLE CHARACTER STUDIES

David: Man after God's Own Heart, Castleman

Elijah, Castleman

Great People of the Bible, Plueddemann

King David: Trusting God for a Lifetime, Castleman

Men Like Us, Heidebrecht & Scheuermann

Paul (Acts 13-28), Christensen

Peter, Castleman

Ruth & Daniel, Stokes

Women Like Us, Barton

Women Who Achieved for God, Christensen

Women Who Believed God, Christensen

Printed in the United States
by Baker & Taylor Publisher Services